BOGEY
BLUES

Tales of Golf Madness

To Jerzy —
May the course be
with you !

Best Wishes
Steve Wilkie
May 1999

BOGEY BLUES

Tales of Golf Madness

Steve Webber

illustrations by

A.B. Frost
from the "Golfer's Alphabet" published in 1898

GRAY EAGLE PUBLISHING
SAN MATEO, CALIFORNIA

Published by:
       Gray Eagle Publishing
       P.O. Box 6905
       San Mateo, CA 94403
       (650) 737-8233

Library of Congress Catalog Card Number: 97-94623
ISBN 1-891407-13-9

Printed by Patterson Printing, Benton Harbor, MI

Book design and production by David Collins.

For Gael

Acknowledgements

Special thanks to Gael Whyte, my partner in life, whose encouragement and editing helped make my insane rambling readable; to David Collins for the time and care taken to bring order to the chaos; and to my brother, Bill English for helping guide me through the process with his advice and enthusiasm.

I'd also like to thank Alta Evangelist, Robert Brown and Ken Castle for their generous help.

And finally, thanks to Frank, Denny, Dave, Don, John, Jimmy and all my golf buddies whose ideas I happily stole.

Table of Contents

The Back Nine

Introduction

These are tales of golf madness.
Bizarre rantings and ravings from a mind that
has been lost in the deep, deep rough.

Beware. You too could be heading down the lonely
cart path to golf insanity. Be warned, golf is no laughing matter.

I know. I once thought I could handle the game. I
was so deep in denial I actually believed I could write
about the anguish of the links. I walked blindly into
the psychic hazards of golf. I began writing short stories for the *San Francisco Chronicle*.

No problem. The game wouldn't take me down.
Sure.

Before long, small cracks in my personality started
to appear on the pages – tiny bits of insanity poked
out among the nouns and verbs. I pushed on,
readers seemed to enjoy my public suffering.

Soon, things got ugly. As my golf game continued in
its nightmare maze of worthless tips, silly swing keys,

vague visualizations, and all the other mental torments I used as I staggered around the links, my mind snapped. The writing went into a darker realm. I was veering off into strange new fairways.

But I didn't care.

By now, I was on a mission. I knew I must tell the world the truth about golf.

So I decided to write this book.

But I needed help. Madmen love company, so I sought out an artist to help me express my dementia. I found my man in a book written in 1898. When I first held this tome I could feel the pain, almost a century old, and it reeked of golf torment. The artist, A.B. Frost, had reached out from the past with his crazed version of the game — it was an omen.

So I wrote this book — *Bogey Blues — Tales of Golf Madness*. Read it before it's too late. Maybe you are not too far gone into the lunacy of the game. Perhaps, *this book can save your life!*

1

To Be or Not To Be

I've found the ultimate golf tip.

And none too soon. I couldn't stand another shank, slice, hook or any unwanted rotation of the golf ball. My world was spinning out of control, I was in the rough and facing the downswing of my life.

That's when I met him.

Phillipe Navarro.

Professional dance instructor by night, he is a sportsman, *bon vivant* and consummate linksman by day. He has style, flair — the air of a man who knows birdies well and has soared with eagles. One who can rumba and tango a golf ball, spinning it at will. Smooth is a crude word when describing Phillipe. Cashmere is straw on his back.

Part French and part Portuguese, he has a Euro-Harvard accent he picked up at Oxford. His golf swing is a dance in the wind. A Navarro practice stroke makes women swoon.

Quite a guy. I should know. I made him up.

You see, I am Phillipe Navarro.

I created him because I had ceased to exist as a golfer. The will was shot. I had gone through countless swing keys, hundreds of tips, thousands of words and I was in the ball washer.

Sure, I had tried the mind stuff. The "Inner Game," "Self One" and "Self Two" and "just let your self do it." Well, none of my selves was doing anything. I didn't need a new swing, another tip, or visualization mumbo jumbo. I needed a whole new guy. A new personality. A fresh start.

> He has style, flair – the air of a man who knows birdies well and has soared with eagles.

I was desperate. A round had been scheduled and I was out of excuses. The tee time was set. The die was cast. But I was melting down. Another ego-slashing round and my mind might go into the wrong fairway for good.

I wasn't going to show. Then it came to me. Of course I wasn't going to show. That was *it*, the small brilliant light, the yin and the yang. I wouldn't show, but I'd *be* there. Just a slight psyche adjustment. Mental sleight of hand.

So simple, so perfect. I would invent a golf persona – a whole new personality to manage the game.

"I've found the secret to the game . . ."

Someone to handle the dirty work. Why should I suffer? Such an inspiration, but the best was yet to come. If I was going to send in a new me, why not go all the way?

From there it was a short leap to Phillipe. I wanted someone with rhythms suited to golf — hence a dancer. I needed courage. Navarro is a bull. Phillipe Navarro would be a name to reckon with.

When I hit the links I would no longer be me — it would be the great Phillipe carrying the bag.

The plan worked to perfection. When I introduced myself as Phillipe, my golf partners hardly raised an eyebrow. Even the accent didn't seem to bother them. They didn't flinch when I yelled "rumba!" after a well-struck ball. Not a snicker when Phillipe executed some classy *bossa nova* moves on the fairway.

It was obvious. Phillipe was a wonderful golf companion. He didn't gripe about the weather, course conditions or some physical ailment. He didn't complain about his job. It was like he was born to play golf. And play he did. He was bold and smooth.

Phillipe was a natural.

So there you have it. A golf career saved. And the best golf tip you'll ever get. If the game gets too rough — give up. You don't have to do it. Develop your own golfing alter ego.

Remember, the game is a lot easier to play if you are not really there . . .

2

Mental Hazards

So what is the hottest new trend in golf?
Jumbo drivers? Whip-like shafts?
Forget it.

If you want to be on the cutting edge of the game, go out and get your own personal sports psychologist.

A golf shrink. A soothing voice to quell the horrors of the game. There is a lot of mental unbalance loose on the fairways and it is time to face the truth.

You need help.

A trained professional can untangle the deep rough of your golf psyche and introduce you to some swell psycho-jargon — "Well, yes, I am having a problem with my putting lately, but my therapist says I'm just trying to work through some old rage."

Let your golf pals chew on that for awhile.

Of course there are some pitfalls to the psychology game. You have to be careful who digs into the sand

Rage is an appropriate response to the game.

trap of your mind. Like anything else, you need a specialist. The following guide will help you decide which therapy is indicated for your particular golf trauma.

Compulsive Hookers

Golfers who can't stop hooking their shots are aggressive people with addictive personalities. They do best when confined. These people lie and are very loud — don't invite them to parties.

Hookers suffer from deep denial. They will blast a ball over the trees and out of bounds and say, "Well, at least I hooked the ball." Hookers aren't in touch with reality.

The first step for any hooker is to admit he has a problem. Even with this willingness, the desire to hook is deeply rooted. Hooking is connected with feelings of masculinity, power and dominance.

The best therapy for hooking appears to be behavior modification. Electric shock treatments administered after every regressive hooking episode seem to help with this horrible affliction. A word of warning — hookers should not try hypnotherapy. A hooker's subconscious is very ugly and should be avoided. Many hookers have found twelve-step programs to be beneficial.

Regressive Slicers

Golfers who slice the ball are insecure, passive people who complain a lot. They are often constipated. Slicers are riddled with guilt. Slicers, unlike hookers, do not suffer from denial. They will admit to anything. They are wrong and they know it. Slicers make fine pets.

These left-to-right spinners have low self-esteem, which translates into an improper release at impact and poor follow through.

The best therapy for these repressed individuals is body work and emotional purging. Primal Therapy or some good hands-on Rolfing can help timid slicers let go and take a truly aggressive swing at the ball. Assertiveness training is also essential to the therapeutic process.

> Slicers, will admit to anything. They are wrong and they know it. Slicers make fine pets.

"If you slice, don't be so nice" is an appropriate axiom for these people pleasers.

The Shame of Poor Putting

I know you don't want to talk about it. It is something nice people don't discuss. You'd rather keep it in the closet. But the truth is, your putter just doesn't seem to work anymore.

Poor putting is an intensely personal issue that involves deep shame and feelings of disgust. The only way to deal with the problem is to face it. Many techniques have been tried to cure poor putting, some of them shocking. Bad putters tend to go from one therapist to another, searching for some "miracle cure." They are prone to dabble in fringe "pop" psychology and New Age thinking. Poor putters are easy prey to con-artists promising a magic solution.

Don't be fooled. Most psychologists now believe poor putting is a sexual dysfunction. With care and compassion a qualified sex therapist can usually help with the disorder. There is no need to hide your putting problems anymore. More and more golfers with the "yips" are seeking help and finally coming to terms with their feelings of shame and guilt. Poor putting is not a disgrace, you are not a bad person — you are sick and it is costing you a lot of strokes. Get help.

I did, and it has done wonders for my game.

I entered the clinic about six months ago and I think my rehab is going well.

I'm still a lousy golfer but I don't seem to care. The medication works great. I've been making excellent progress at the miniature golf course at the institution and my therapist says I may get to play with my big clubs again real soon.

3

Bad Lies

Yes, there is a massive cover-up.
Do you think the government wants you to
know the truth about golf?
No way.
They're scared.

The government is afraid of widespread panic
and chaos if the facts about golf ever became public.
They are hiding the evidence. Informed sources have
disclosed the existance of secret files, unexplained
photographs, and even some golf objects made out
of materials that don't exist on this planet. Some say
the CIA has a hidden body of an alien golfer, before
it took human form.

Absurd?

Insane?

Perhaps. At this time, much of what I'm about to
reveal is just theory, but one thing is for certain.

Golf is strange.

Where did it come from? Why is it here? Why won't it go away? Here are some theories:

Professional Golfers

The people you see playing golf on television are not human. They are aliens from a distant solar system who have invaded our planet and plan to drive earth-beings totally insane. They have been sent to spread golf, like a plague, to every corner of the globe.

Their mission is simple. Make golf look easy, lure the unsuspecting into the game, and watch them go mad.

Then, take over the earth.

Their plan is working.

Top levels of every government on the planet have been infiltrated with golf. Many of our leaders have already been driven insane by the game. Soon, there will be outbreaks of random violence, and eventually, war. Battles will be fought for prime golf course land. Golfers will run amuck.

The leaders of the invasion are the PGA Tour members. They are *all* spacemen. This is really not that hard to detect. The leader of the aliens, Jack Nicklaus, is obviously not from this planet. Have you ever seen his eyes? Scary. He could easily bore holes in you with a mere glance. It is best not to let professional golfers look at you, and of course, don't ever watch them. They are here to humiliate us and make us weak.

The invasion of the Tour members is nearing

completion. Recently, they have sent their ultimate weapon. The destroyer of minds has arrived. Tiger Woods, the supreme ruler of the aliens, is here to finish the job. Much has been said about the talent and maturity of this young golfer – this is no wonder considering that by my calculations he is about 600 years old and has been playing golf on his home planet for over five centuries. Remember, you will *never* look like a pro, much less a Tiger Woods. They are playing with your mind. They want you to think you can play, so maybe you'll head for the . . .

Golf is strange. Where did it come from? Why is it here? Why won't it go away?

Driving Range

Welcome to hell.

Here, rows of hapless victims hit golf balls in a pinball like frenzy of useless activity. Cursing and whining, they splay shots wildly in a vain attempt to find the hidden "key" to the game.

Well, if there is a "key" the aliens aren't about to let you know it. The driving ranges are run by the invaders. They control everything. There are force-fields which control ball flight. Nothing is as it seems.

Ever wonder why you can hit the ball so well at

All golf equipment is made in Outer Space.

the range and then turn into a spineless wonder on the links?

The aliens love to see you suffer.

They use the range to blind you to reality.

They give you false hope. But soon, after a few soul crushing rounds, the shame becomes unbearable and you *will* seek out the . . .

Golf Pro

These are the storm troopers of the alien invasion. They are here to break the will of earthlings. Back on their home planet they are mind control experts trained in the art of brainwashing. Golf pros attack the left-side of the brain, destroying your ability to reason. They *do* know the secret of the swing, but they aren't going to tell you.

Golf pros divulge just enough details to keep you dazed and confused. Soon your mind will become blank and you will be easy prey for whatever suggestions the pro plants in your subconscious.

You will begin to have periods of depression, black-outs and thoughts of suicide.

The pro will also introduce you to an amazing battery of devices to play the game. Let's check out the . . .

Equipment

All golf clubs and balls are made in outer space. They do not conform to the laws of gravity or physics.

They don't work.

Everyone knows that golf clubs automatically twist

in your hand at impact, and that all putters shake with some mysterious vibration. The aliens have built small undetectable devices into the equipment to ruin your game. The balls are programmed to spin into pre-selected energy fields, such as sand and water.

There is no hope, you will fail.

You may wonder how I know all of this. Well, I've seen the aliens. I was out playing golf by myself one day and I had just missed another two-footer, when I felt something sort of snap.

Next thing I know, I'm in this spaceship and these guys wearing fuzzy sweaters were standing over me mumbling something about divots. It felt like they were implanting something in my brain.

I don't remember anything more until I woke up lying in a sand trap. Now I'm waiting for them to come back. I know they're after me. But I don't care. Because in that spaceship I learned the truth. The secret of the game. A voice whispered in my ear. It said:

"Give up."

4

A Star Is Born

Some things you should never see. One of them is your golf swing.

Deep in our hacker's hearts we actually think we look good swinging a club. We are smooth. We are graceful. We are happy in our delusion.

But sometimes reality slips in like a back door putt.

I had been in a slight six-year slump with my game. Nothing serious. I did have to take a nap after every round to blot out the humiliation, but the depression usually lasted only a couple of days.

Like I said, nothing serious.

Still, I decided to confront my golf demons — stare them in the eye. So I took a video golf lesson. Maybe this wasn't the wisest decision for someone with a obsessive/compulsive personality. One moment I'm just your average linkster with a slight depressive disorder, the next, I'm an addict — a twisted, range-ball junkie.

I went downhill fast. I saw myself on tape and that was it. It was exhilarating. Sure, I looked like a clown on the screen, but also I saw for the first time the truth — the answer. I could actually see my terrible golfing wrongs.

After the lesson, armed with my new knowledge, I hit a bucket of balls. They flew majestically into the night sky. White points of light, soaring in triumph.

I was a star.

The ecstasy lasted about ten hours. Near dawn I was back at the range, my blood rushing with anticipation. I wanted

I would lock myself in a darkened room. I watched the tapes over and over. Slow motion. Freeze frame. Over and over . . .

more. But, of course, it was gone, the groove had slipped silently away in my sleep. Stolen. I hit my usual assortment of erratic shots. I was crushed.

I felt like a shank.

So the cycle started. I would take a lesson and the glory would come back. For awhile I soared, but then came the inevitable crash. Soon, I became a pitiful creature, lurking around the outer mats at the range, hunched over, my eyes full of fear and dread.

The video tapes of my lessons chronicled my total collapse as a human being. I got uglier and nastier on every tape. The sessions were digging deeper and

We know our golf swings are smooth and graceful . . .

deeper into my fragile golf psyche. I became foul and dangerous looking.

After my lessons, I would lock myself in a darkened room. Armed with my remote control, I watched the tapes over and over. Slow motion. Freeze frame. Over and over.

I only left my room to go to the range. Daylight began to hurt my eyes and I started squinting when I went outdoors. I looked like a mole.

My friends thought I was getting a little strange. A bit strung out.

I guess they thought they were helping. I was at the range, and yes, it was 4 a.m. and pitch black, but I was almost getting *it*. I was chipping balls off the mat, humming to myself. I was dressed in my bathrobe and maybe I hadn't shaved for a few days. But I was getting *close*. I was just swinging the club back and forth, back and forth, back and forth — I was almost *there*.

They gently took my club and led me away from the mat. I plopped down on the putting green. I felt like an unreplaced divot.

It was over.

They took my tapes away.

But I fooled them. You see, I was very *close*. I was right *there*.

What they don't know is that I don't *need* the tapes. I can still see my swing in my mind and someday *I will* find *it*. I just have to sit here and watch myself swing, over and over and over . . .

5

"You Da Man"

When I was a kid the only people who played golf were the fathers on the family sitcoms – Ozzie Nelson, Beaver's dad, Fred Mac Murray in "My Three Sons" – a bunch of guys in alpaca sweaters who didn't have jobs.

Well, things have changed.

Golf is everywhere and there is no place to hide.

Someday, a person of importance – a boss, client or future father-in-law – is going to ask you to play a "casual round." Sure. Remember this – *there is no such thing as a casual round.*

You will be watched. Probed. Dissected. Your whole life will be judged by your golf game. Can you handle pressure? Are you a choke? What is your pain threshold?

It's all there.

Take the drive.

If you can't hit the ball straight, you are out of control and potentially dangerous. If you push the ball — a weak shot to the right — you can't to be trusted and are probably a whiner. The silent embezzler type. If you pull the ball hard to the left you are obnoxious, a lout and probably a drunk. A wife stealer. If you can't putt, everyone knows you can't close a deal and will eventually cost the firm big bucks.

So what to do?

Well, obviously you'll never be able to play golf well enough to impress anyone. Your game will always be an embarrassment. The best tactic is to try and draw attention away from your horrible play. Fake it. Put up a good front.

———————◆———————

You will be watched. Probed. Dissected. Your whole life will be judged by your golf game.

———————◆———————

Here are some tips:

Dress

The big thing on the pro circuit is endorsements. Logos on your hat, sweater, shirt, bag, etc. This is a good image. It makes you appear important. The best bet is to try to look like a human billboard. Logos all over the place, bag tags from exotic courses you've never even seen, and assorted tournament badges dangling around your neck.

Tell people you have a sponsor.

The endorsement thing can actually work. Recently, I got a letter and a check from a company whose logo I display prominently, offering me a small fee not to have their name anywhere near me.

Nicknames

Your own name isn't good enough for the links. You need something with a little dash. Even if you can't play, adopt a moniker that implies you are awesome. Animals are good. Bear, Shark, Walrus, etc. seem to work. Obviously, Tiger Woods is the ultimate name for a golfer. Variations on the theme might be the way to go — Wildcat Wedge, Cougar Chipper, Panther Putter, Lion Iron.

Once you have your nickname, it is *very* important to always refer to yourself in the third person. Never, ever, say I. Always refer to yourself like you are someone else.

"Boy, did you see the shot Wildcat just made?"

"Cougar likes birdies."

If someone asks you what score you got on a hole say, "Panther got his par."

Your golf buddies will think this is very cool.

Accessories

Since you can't play golf, don't confine yourself to the tools of the game. Bring other toys. Electronics are hip. Bring the cell phone and use it. You are in demand. A personal computer on the golf cart shows some style

It is more important to act cool than to play well.

and a portable fax machine makes a statement. A loud beeper will get your partner's attention.

A boom box on the golf cart is cool. Rap, grunge and heavy metal can really liven up those long, quiet fairways.

Playing

Fake it. Act cool. Practice leaning against your club with your legs crossed, without falling. Do everything in slow motion.

Take your time. Golfers respect this.

Stand behind your ball for a good 20 seconds lining up your shot. Squat down. Peer into the distance. Back off. Take another look.

Ignore fidgeting or comments of others. Do your own thing. Address the ball. Again, back off and take about five slow practice swings. Re-address the ball. Waggle the club. Bob your head up and down. Look intense. Start the club back slowly — then suddenly move away, saying, "It just doesn't feel right." Repeat procedure.

Golfers will admire your serious approach to the game.

Drinking

Touchy subject. Booze used to be an important part of the game. The idea was, if you were really any good, you could play blind. If you can drink, and play, great. That's Bogie. As in Humphrey. If you can't, that's Billy. As in Martin. The best idea is to confuse your playing partners. If you are sober, act drunk. If you are blasted, maintain. Keep them guessing. If you do happen to find yourself so tanked you can barely talk, just say over and over, "You da man."

Gambling

Show courage. Take any bet. Never take any strokes. You're a damn fine golfer, and you'll back it up with your wallet.

Negative wagering will go over well. Like, "I'll bet you five bucks you hit it in the lake." This shows your aggressive stance and will surely impress.

Well, that's it. You're ready to hit the links. You'll be cool.

If you follow the above advice, and bring a nice fat wallet to the course, you're sure to make a lot of new golf buddies.

You can bet on it.

6

Shanks A Lot

Be afraid.
Be very afraid.
Because they are out there.

Waiting.

The unspeakable terror, the shocking horror, the nightmare of the links is coming soon, to a course near you.

Yes.

The Shanks are alive!

And they are after you. You think you can escape, don't you? You think the shanks can't get you.

Not with your sound golf swing.

Silly fool.

You actually believe shanks are caused by some swing defect. You're not afraid. You know if you start shanking the ball you can easily cure yourself of this tiny hiccup in your grooved game.

Forget it.

You can't fix a ghost. When it comes to shanks, you can lose your golf pro — you're gonna need a witch doctor.

Because shanks aren't a golf problem. They are a freak of nature — a disaster, like an earthquake, tornado or the plague. The horrible truth is — *shanks create themselves.*

They are living, breathing entities, that lurk everywhere, just waiting to creep in and destroy your game.

What else could explain this horror? You assume your normal stance, check the target, waggle, take a nice slow backswing, move gracefully into the hitting zone, and out of nowhere the ball whines off the clubface on a flight path of chaos.

> You can't fix a ghost. When it comes to shanks, you can lose your golf pro — you're gonna need a witch-doctor . . .

Whoa. What happened here? You look around. You feel fear, confusion, you're somewhat disoriented. There is, of course, a huge ugly *silence.* Eyes shift to the ground. Nobody knows you.

A shank has you. By association, you, too, are a shank. You have created a monster, the lowest life-form on the links. You are a golf Dr. Frankenstein.

But it really wasn't your fault.

A shank is the lowest life-form on the links.

You're a victim.

I know. I recently suffered a shank attack. The demon shot took over my game and I began firing bullets to the right like a machine-gun. I was dangerous, a golf terrorist – soon my fellow duffers began to avoid me.

I became an outcast.

I tried to "cure" my errant shots. I called a local golf pro. When I told him about the shanks, he told me never to say that word again, because there is no such thing, and hung up. Before long, the shanks started to effect more than just my golf game. My hands started shaking, my voice quivered and I didn't want to leave my room. I needed help.

I saw the notice in the newspaper, next to the hair transplant ads: *Shank No More,* it read. I was saved. I made an appointment and saw the doctor. He explained the relatively safe and simple procedure.

The surgery is ingenious – the first session fuses the left wrist into a permanent straight line and the second phase freezes the neck, so the head can't swivel. Of course, after the surgery, you can no longer drive a car and you have to be very careful crossing the street – but the shanks would be gone.

Fair enough. I set a date for the surgery. No way the shanks were going to beat me. I felt free. I soon would be shankless. I felt so good I decided to play a round of golf – what did I care if I shanked all over the place? The nightmare would soon be over.

A strange thing happened. I was hitting my usual

assortment of gut-wrenching shanks until the fourth hole. On that short dog-leg, my playing partner had an easy 70-yard pitch to the pin. He lined up the shot, took a smooth backswing, moved nicely into the hitting zone and then suddenly the ball screamed off to the right like a bullet.

He froze. There was silence. He looked around, confused. My eyes went quickly to the ground. Yuck, this guy has the shanks – no way I know him.

Funny thing. I didn't shank another shot the entire round. My buddy was firing them to the right like Rush Limbaugh.

Well, that was about a month ago. I still haven't shanked a shot. My pal is doing better, he is recovering well from the surgery, but I'm getting a little tired of driving him everywhere and having to help him cross the street . . .

7

Make Par Not War

Golf is like a black hole.

Sooner or later, the game will suck you in. There is no escape.

I know. I've long ago given up any pretense that I'm in control. Golf runs my life and I accept this.

I'm a sheep. Just herd me down the fairway with the rest of the flock.

I don't care anymore.

I'm never going to stop. No matter how much the game torments and ridicules me, I'm coming back. Heap on the abuse, it doesn't matter, I'll see you on the first tee.

I no longer need a reason to play. I need an excuse.

A good excuse. The old ones seem a bit lame. Fresh air, exercise, companionship, relaxation, sure, fine, but this kind of drivel doesn't carry much weight when I'm in my post-round catatonic state and I can't lift my head off the couch.

I need *big* excuses.

So, I've come up with some perfectly sound rationalizations on why playing golf is a noble, almost heroic undertaking. The next time someone gets in your face about the wisdom of hitting the links, trot out one of the following:

Golf Runs the Economy

"The Hogan Curve," used by many Wall Street insiders, proves without a doubt, that if I stopped playing golf, the world would plunge into a horrible depression. The game is such a perfect waste of time, it is the balancing point for the economy in this country.

Golf is totally unproductive.

Therein lies its beauty and symmetry. There is no good without evil, no pleasure without pain, no prosperity without golf.

If we stopped puttering around on the links, it is estimated the increased productivity would put 7 million people out of work.

I care too much for my country not to help. So I play golf. I read, practice and blab incessantly about the game. Because of golf, I'm throwing away a large part of my life.

And I'm proud of it.

I'm helping the capitalist system survive. As far as I'm concerned, if you don't golf, you're a communist. So the next time some "pinko" gets in your face about "wasting time" on the links, let the tears well up in

Sooner, or later, you will surrender.

your eyes, hum "America the Beautiful" and tell him you are helping keep the free enterprise system well and functioning.

Golf Secures World Peace

The game of golf is war. You attack the course. You launch small projectiles into the air, aimed at a target. You use field tactics and an arsenal of weapons called "clubs" to march down the fairways like an advancing army. Golf is not a kinder, gentler game. It's tough out there.

Golf tests your mettle. It's a gut check to see if you have the right stuff. Playing golf simulates combat. It's the perfect way to sublimate our violent inner nature.

> Golf is a religion and we should get a tax break on green fees.

All great warmongers love golf. They get to boom one down the fairway, sink a putt and blast out of bunkers.

Without golf, many world leaders would have to "act out" their aggressions and create real wars. I say let all the soldiers tee it up, and let's put an end to global violence.

Make *par*, not *war*.

Golf Improves Mental Health

This is a tricky one, but it works. If you watch golfers during a round, you might think this is a very sick game played by emotionally stunted people. This, of course, is true. But is that bad? Could it be that this disturbing game is the perfect tonic for the hapless neurotic? I know it has done wonders for me.

During a round of golf I get to sample the entire menu of emotional responses. For an appetizer, I shank a wedge and feel despair. The next course might be a duck-hook into the woods and a fine feeling of rage. The entree could be a hot burning slice into the next fairway and the accompanying sense of humiliation. And for dessert, perhaps the icy chilling fear of a downhill two-foot putt.

By the time I've completed a round, I've had a full rich slice of life. Who needs to worry about work, relationships, kids, bills and other nonsense, when you're staring down a tight fairway with water to the left and OB on the right? Golf is more real than reality.

Golf is Spiritual

Golf is a religion and I think we should get a tax break on green fees. The major doctrine of Golf is the total domination and humiliation of the hacker. Through the practice of Golf the ego structure of the duffer is soon shattered and he begins to learn the lesson of humility. It can be a painful experience.

Many golfers have strong defense mechanisms and are deep into denial. They struggle mightily to master the game. They want to control their golf destiny. They want to be bigger than the game.

Sometimes it takes years, or even decades, but sooner or later the entire personality of the golfer will be destroyed. This is a profound Zen-like experience that can totally transform a person. Many golfers, having had this catharsis, give up their former meaningless pursuit of earthly pleasures and spend the rest of their lives as caddies.

The spiritual aspect of golf is a noble reason to hit the links. It's a fine excuse for teeing it up on Sundays.

So, now you have some rational motives for your golf obsession. You are not some fanatic fairway freak – you are an upstanding, concerned, giving, patriotic humanitarian.

Bless you.

8

Duffer's Inferno

I've been to hell and back.

Many times.

The nightmare journey is not far away. It's as close as the nearest driving range.

This is the home of tortured souls, dashed dreams and lost hopes. It is a wretched, evil place haunted by the living dead. At the range, strange, unearthly sounds fill the air — high-pitched whines of golf balls spinning wildly out of control — and the low moans of the madmen who inhabit this bleak domain. Here, in this pit of pain, the suffocating presence of total defeat and humiliation is so thick you could drink it like a milkshake. Doom hangs in the air.

I love the driving range.

But, of course, I'm mad.

We all know how the driving range lures its victims — how the vicious cycle begins. It's been a few days

The driving range is hell . . .

since your last round of golf and the trauma is slowly
starting to wane. The memory of the tightly clenched
jaw and the sick, queasy feeling in your stomach is
starting to fade. Sure, you said you'd never be back.
You were tired of the mental whipping at the hands of
this merciless game.

You were through.

Then the golf magazine came in the mail.

You didn't open it for a couple of days. To hell with
golf. But you couldn't help noticing the blazing head-
line – "CURE YOUR SLICE IN ONE LESSON."
Hmmmm, if you could just stop slicing, maybe you
could live with the topped shots, bladed chips, pulled
irons and the occasional duck-hook.

So you take a peek. Why, of course, it's so simple,
no wonder you're slicing the ball, it says right here
you're casting from the top and throwing the swing
plane on an outside path, which spins the ball left-to-
right. What a dumb guy. There are pictures that show
you what you are doing wrong and how to correct the
problem. Well, adiós Mr. Slice.

Presto. Gone. Cured.

One of the symptoms of golf insanity is a total lack
of recall; a mental defense system that completely
blocks out the past. Somehow, one forgets that perhaps
this process has occurred before, once, or twice, or
maybe a few hundred times? Humiliating round, quit
the game, new tip, solve the problem. Sound familiar?
Probably not, because you are in deep denial and a
very sick person.

So with reality firmly hidden in some dark closet of your mind, hope fills your heart.

You believe.

Brother, how you believe.

You are so certain that your slice is gone, you call your golfing buddies to tell them the news.

You're back.

And you know you have this game licked.

There is just one tiny detail left. Nothing major. Really just a formality.

You need a quick trip to the driving range to see your "new" swing in action.

Somewhere, the devil is laughing.

> The only sound is the clacking of spikes, like tiny hoofs of cattle being led off to slaughter.

He's got you again and you're heading for hell.

The next day, you get up early, you are filled with anticipation. You are a new person. You have been saved. You can't wait for the "other losers" at the range to see your "new" swing. You are no longer like them, with their pathetic slices — you are special.

When you arrive at the range you are so focused, you neglect to see the same glazed, slightly maniacal look in the eyes of the other range addicts. Of course, everyone read the same magazine.

They all believe.

Eyes wide, everyone staggers through the morning

mist. Like zombies, the group descends on the ball machine. No one speaks. The only sound is the clacking of spikes, like tiny hoofs of cattle being led off to slaughter.

The horror is about to begin.

Balls are teed up.

One by one, shots soar into the morning air. They are magnificent displays of golf perfection – not a slice to be seen – strong, straight shots, some with a slight draw. You look quickly around to catch the admiring glances of your buddies, but everyone is so focused, they see only their own shots. So what, you think. They can see the next one or the one after that.

More balls are teed up.

A strange thing happens. From the far edge of the range a shrill whine fills the air as a horrible, twisted, spinning slice cuts across the entire hitting area. Everyone freezes. The sky seems to darken, the mood subtly shifts, confusion and doubt seem to descend.

Soon, more slices are screaming through the air and a low moan of despair echoes through the range. One by one, the zombies abandon their "new" swing and are desperately trying to find ways to "work" with their awful slice.

You wallow in your torment until your bucket of balls dwindles down. Your slice is working to perfection, and you are even achieving a painful stinging sensation at impact. Without hope, you line up your last ball.

The devil smiles.

You hit the most awesome drive of your life, it starts out right and gracefully spins back down the middle and rolls to the far fence – a place your balls never visit.

You stand frozen.

It's a miracle – you have seen the light. You *know* you can play this game.

You *believe*.

So you get another bucket of balls.

And the devil laughs.

9

Prime Time

"**M**anny, yeah it's Barry. Listen, we gotta talk. I've got concepts, Manny. I'm hot. I'm on fire over here.

"Look, work with me on this, Manny. What I want you to do is put me on the speaker phone, lean back and relax.

"Ready?

"O.K. Close your eyes. I've got one word for you.

"*Golf.*

"You see it Manny?

"Stay with me on this. Think *trend*. Think *ratings*.

"You see it?

"I'm seeing network, I'm seeing major stars, I'm seeing prime time. We've got thirty, maybe forty million hackers out there. Waiting. They're dying for it babe, they want it and they want it all. And kid, who better than me, the duff-man himself, Barry Links, to give it to them. I'm a TV producer who breathes golf. I know what these people need.

"Action.

"Something new, something big — golf with a flair — the Barry Flair. I mean, you've got your golf channel, tournaments, interviews, hey, who needs it? Golf is a monster, golf is a ratings Godzilla. Golf is *now,* new formats, new concepts. I see golf, I see wide open, endless fairways of dead-solid Nielsons.

"You follow me? Demographics. Hey, just off the top of my head, let me chip up a few concepts — I see tap-in putts to the Emmys here.

"First I think we need to bring Geraldo in on this golf thing. He's baby-boom — he bridges the gap from the country club to the public courses. We did lunch the other day. Boy, this guy is out there. He actually believes a certain element of the golf community has gone over the edge and is into some cult worship trip. Geraldo, I love this guy. He's totally nuts. But what do we care? We'll give him a crew, a camera and watch him bleed.

"We'll send him undercover to 'expose' the golf menace and if we're lucky, Geraldo will get in some duffer's face and take a nine-iron to the nose. Great stuff. Super video.

"Next we need a show to get the golf humor thing working. We go with a no-brainer. A sitcom called *'The Sand Trap'* about a 19th hole cocktail lounge at some funky country club. Ripoff-wise we're talking 'Cheers' with the golf thing happening. The bartender is a

On the golf soap opera "Buried Lies," things are heating up.

burnt out former golf pro. Get the drift? The local barfly duffers idolize him. Let's not even fool around, I see Frazier, Sam, Coach, Carla, Norm, Cliff – we'll change the names and steal them all. Lots of stupid golf jokes, heavy boozing and tons of sexual innuendos.

"And for a kicker, we get this Chi Chi Rodriquez fella – I hear he's a scream – to do a cameo as a bartender. Here's the best part. Nobody in the bar knows who he is. So Chi Chi mugs for the camera, drops a few pearls about golf and everybody in the bar ignores him. Of course the audience knows

I'm just taking big wild swing here, but I think Trevino could be the next Oprah.

it's Chi Chi, so they go crazy whenever he does any stuff. Chi Chi's got the great hat and he can throw in his famous club waving bit – I gotta believe we're talking top-ten here.

"Women are getting into the golf thing big time. We target them with a daytime soap, 'Buried Lies,' the seedy, sexy, steamy underbelly of golf. Trent Par, owner of the ultra exclusive 'Hidden Fairways Private Golf Resort,' oversees the daily lives of the members and guests as they intermingle life on the links with their sordid affairs, boozing, cheating, multiple personalities, murder and whatever else the sicko writers can think up.

"I've shopped the concept. I've got a network go and sponsors begging to jump on.

"We need a hot new show for the prime time slot. I'm thinking a hard-hitting cop/golf drama thing called *PGA Blues*. Lots of violence, mayhem, I like the jumpy camera, fast-paced look. The thing is, we mix in the rules of golf with all the gore. Each week we slip some obscure golf rule into the plot. Golfers will eat it up. I see a partner/buddy thing, a couple of down-on-their-luck former golf pros who go undercover on the PGA tour and solve golf-related crimes. I hear the tour guys are into all sorts of stuff, really wild, so we've got tons of material. Killer ratings.

"I may be going out on a limb here, but I think Lee Trevino has something special. People love the guy They open up to him. I'm just taking a big wild swing here, but I think Trevino could be the next Oprah.

"Daytime talk is happening. We plug in the golf angle, we get Lee, and bingo — adiós, Oprah. We get some weird guests to come on to tell their most embarrassing golf stories. Lee jokes with them, next thing you know they are spilling their guts and the audience goes crazy. A gimme Daytime Emmy for Lee.

"Manny, am I hot or what? I'm a human flamethrower. I think you gotta believe we're going to own prime time. I'm thinking we need a major push here, jump on this golf thing big time. Talk to me about the TV line-up and get your people with the program, let's bang out some stuff and we'll go with a total media blitz. Work with me on this Manny, put together a package and get back to me. I need feedback Manny, input, concepts . . ."

10

Fast Green

FAX

TO: BARRY, PRESIDENT LINKS PRODUCTIONS

FROM: MANNY, WORLDWIDE MEDIA INC.

RE.: GOLF

Barry – you're beautiful. Loved your TV links
concepts. Agree golf is a monster. We see market
saturation to coincide with your new fall line-up.
Have projects in pipeline. Advise on following:

"The Iron Man"
A blockbuster film starring Sylvester Stallone as Jake, a
blind caddie from Queens who trains at night and

qualifies for the U.S. Open. Jake faces overwhelming competition from a foreign contingent of golfers headed by the evil Divot, a huge Romanian golfer. Played by Marlon Brando, Divot routinely drives the ball well over 400 yards. It's a tale of good against evil, power versus the short game. Box office gold.

Clackaphobia, the dread of hearing golf spikes scrapping on cement, has claimed countless victims.

"Hackers"

A golf zombie terrorizes a quiet country club. A movie that taps into the drive-in movie demographic. Basic slasher motif. A demented psycho lurches around doing some serious damage with his driver. No plot. Black and white. Sparse dialogue. A violent golf exploitation film with a pseudo artistic look. Low budget, huge profits.

"Duffer"

Concept golf album by Michael Jackson. The "Thriller" thing but we plug in the links. Golf ballads, hip hop, pop, rock and even a little rap. "Gonna be shootin' Birdies," "Baby, this is a Bad Lie," "Sink it," that sort of thing. Video tie-in with Michael blending dance moves with the golf swing. Also a tap dance number in golf spikes, tuxedo and a club instead of a cane. A chip shot to a Grammy.

Fear is rampant on the links . . .

"Eat To Birdie" — This is a fast-paced, hard-hitting nutritional guide for golfers. In this controversial potential best-seller, Dr. Harvey Platinum outlines his food-word-imagery diet.

"If you want birdies, eat 'em," he preaches. Platinum has golfers follow a diet based completely on fowl. After 14 days of eating poultry you will lower your handicap by ten strokes, according to the Platinum Research Center. For vegetarian golfers, the Center recommends eggs.

"Terror on the Course"
This book deals with the fear that is rampant on the fairways. The popularity of golf has given rise to a rash of hacker-related phobias. A recent article in *Medical Monthly* focuses on this growing problem and its various manifestations.

Alpacaphobia, the fear of sweaters, heads a long list of maladies. Clackaphobia, the dread of hearing golf spikes scrapping on cement, has claimed countless victims. Gripopia, the fear of leather golf gloves that stiffen into hideous shapes and hide in the dark recesses of the golf bag, is another common link terror. The book is not pleasant reading, but it could offer help for the truly afflicted.

"Beyond Golf"
A metaphysical view of what golf really means. Written by Carl. Carl is one with golf. Carl tells of his lifelong quest for enlightenment through his clubs. In fact, the characters in his book are his clubs. The

driver, named Ed, is seeking truth. The putter, Sam, already knows, and the sand wedge is at the beach. Deep reading for link purists.

END FAX:
BARRY – GOLF IS GOLD. YOU'RE BEAUTIFUL.

11

Dead in the Hole

The reason you can't putt is simple.

You fear death.

Forget all the stuff about accelerating the club-head, a longer/shorter backswing, or making sure your left wrist doesn't breakdown.

It's all nonsense.

You're afraid of the black hole.

The void.

The nothingness.

The end.

Death.

Watching the ball disappear into the unknown of the dark hole triggers a primitive survival response – the seemingly small act of sinking a putt, reminds you of your mortality. Seeing the white light of the golf ball fade into blackness, chills your soul.

You are secretly terrified of making putts.

And it gets worse as we get older.

Younger golfers can boldly stroke the ball into the cup because they have no fear of death. They think they will live forever. They are dumb.

Older, seasoned duffers, are wise enough to know the end is near. Anything that remotely reminds us of this fact is to be avoided at all costs.

Seeing the golf ball swallowed into the abyss isn't always a welcomed sight. No wonder you get the yips. Who wouldn't get a little jumpy, facing the end?

———————◆———————

Seeing the white light of the golf ball, fade into blackness, chills our soul.

———————◆———————

So what can you do?

The first step in overcoming your fear of putting is to face the truth and stop the denial.

Quit making excuses.

"I opened the putter blade, I looked up, my ball hit a spike mark, blah, blah."

Give it up.

You yanked the putt because you are scared. You don't want to see the little ball disappear, because you don't want to disappear.

Golfers tend to see the golf ball as extensions of themselves. If the ball falls into the black hole, they are right behind it, cascading into the unknown.

Understanding this relationship with the ball can help you conquer your fear. Don't be afraid to talk to

We are secretly terrified of making putts.

your ball. Let the ball know you feel its pain and terror. Share your anxieties with the ball. Open up. Create a dialogue – build trust.

One way to communicate with your golf ball is to understand how the ball feels. One method I find effective is the barrel drill. Find yourself a large barrel and sit in it. Imagine you are a golf ball lying at the bottom of the cup. It's a dark, lonely, terrifying place. Practice sitting in the barrel for long periods of time and slowly it will become less scary and you may experience a feeling of peace and tranquility. You are facing the void. You are staring the bottom of the cup in the eye.

Once you have faced your fears, you learn the truth.

To make a putt, you have to be willing to die.

Say to yourself.

"To sink this three-foot putt I'm willing to enter the vast nothingness of the unknown and have my body turn to dust."

Make the commitment.

Be brave.

You will make those short putts.

Or die trying.

12

Links Lemmings

F ace the truth.

Golf is the most important thing in life.

When you are on your game, you feel large, huge — a monster capable of ruling the planet. You love yourself. But when your game crumbles, you feel small, worthless, confused and frightened. You know you should be punished.

You are a slave to the game.

Golf owns you.

But why?

Why is golf *everything?*

Most duffers believe there is no "why" to golf. Golf just is. They surrender to the game and seem to accept the fact that you don't choose golf — golf chooses you. The game is the master and like links lemmings we stagger down countless fairways and leap blindly to our doom.

But is it possible that there is some tangible reason why golf rules our existence?

Is there a why?

Currently there are teams of scientists working on various hypothesis to explain the golf epidemic. Many believe golf is part of an alien invasion *(see chapter three)* but recent discoveries have given credence to the following theories:

> They surrender to the game and seem to accept the fact that you don't choose golf – golf chooses you.

Gene Pool Theory

This theory proposes that the desire to play golf is a genetic defect. Probably passed through the male chromosome, a mutation has developed which predisposes one to the golf disorder. Studies on identical twins seem to support this theory. The following test has been devised to detect the defective gene. Answer yes or no, to the following:

1. Does your father play golf? Do any members of your family (brothers, sisters, aunts, uncles, grandparents) golf?

2. Do you ever golf first thing in the morning?

3. Have you ever tried to quit the game and failed?

4. Do you take mulligans?

If you answer yes to any of the above questions, and of course you did, you may have a defective golf gene. You will suffer great pain.

The Darwin Effect

Here, we trace golf back to the time of cavemen. We know our early ancestors were avid duffers from the discovery of fossil golf clubs. Of course, by today's standards, the equipment was somewhat crude; but it appears the cavemen understood the basic concept of loft to flight ratio, and some rather impressive drivers and irons have turned up. The balls, naturally, were made of stone, which did limit distance, but it appears these primitive linksmen put a premium on accuracy.

Actually, the game was somewhat different during this period, in that the object was to hit prey with the shot rather than aim at a stationary target. Score was kept by how many shots it took to get dinner.

The discovery of ancient drawings found in pre-historic caves seems to indicate that our ancestors viewed golf much as we do today.

These primitive etchings paint a picture of frustration: drawings of different swing techniques, pictures of strong and weak grips, open stance, closed stance — the images portray the nightmare of the game staring back at us from the dawn of time.

So what does this mean?

It could be that golf is encoded in us as a primitive

A pre-historic golfer hunting for food . . .

survival tool. Early duffers played because they needed to eat.

Is it possible that we are acting out some ancient hunting ritual that has survived millions of years of evolution? Are we nothing more than cavemen, bashing about with our clubs in search of a little grub?

We've all seen golfers driven to such a frenzy on the course, that they look quite capable of killing small prey, if it ventured by, so there just may be some validity to this theory.

Duffer's Disease

This theory explains golf from a medical perspective – the game is a disease. Golf is a virus. It is an illness much like measles, chicken pox or the black plague. The disease model does explain why such vast numbers are affected, (or infected) with the golf bug.

Also, long term exposure to the game does seem to cause brain damage, which eventually turns the afflicted into a babbling, incoherent bore.

Golf does seem to be catchy. Hang around duffers long enough and their constant chattering about the game seems to make people sick. The reaction seems to be either avoidance of the game or succumbing to the golf disease. It may be that some people have a built in immunity to golf, while others are easy prey to the deadly virus.

Presently, all major theories on why golf is taking over the planet have one major theme – we're doomed. It appears quite possible that golf will end civilization as we know it.

The one fact that stands out in all the studies, seems to seal our fate:

Golf always wins.

13

'Le Mondo' Golf

We all know golf isn't a hobby — it's a second job.

If you want to keep up, you're going to need extensive training.

That's why hackers don't take vacations — they go to summer school. Golfers pack up their clubs and head out to a golf institute, academy or clinic.

For the truly committed golfer, may I suggest my own newly-opened golf enrichment experience — the fabulous Le Mondo Inner Memory Golfing Club.

This is no ordinary golf camp. At Le Mondo we are "le different." We swing to the beat of the inner-duffer. We don't teach golf — we become it.

At Le Mondo we do not believe in professional instructors. What do they know? We feel everyone is a teacher, so we practice the revolutionary concept of having our guests coach each other. Your roommate is your pro. Think of all the fun you will have arguing about the correct grip, stance, swing plane, leg, hip, arm, wrist action and other keen stuff you have gleaned from the latest golf magazine.

Another exclusive Mondo feature is the lack of a golf course. For the mental work we do, an actual golf layout would be too cumbersome, heavy and vague. We don't believe you actually have to play golf to improve your game. How you "feel" you would play, if you could, is our barometer of success.

Sometimes way down deep, we *know* we are better golfers than we *think* we are.

If, through our innovative inner memory program, you see yourself as a better golfer, we say you are.

But enough of Mondo Theory. Let's check out an average day at the club.

8 a.m. – Coffee and bragging. This gives club members the opportunity to really start slinging it as they crank up for the day. Show-and-tell is encouraged. Bring all your trumped-up scorecards from the famous courses you have visited but never played.

9 a.m. – Tee time. The real meat of the Mondo Theory begins at this verbal free-for-all where guests explain their vast knowledge of the game to each other. Rare insights,

Putting for chow at "Le Mondo Inner Memory Golfing Club"

along with the occasional fist fight, high-light this spirited session.

Noon – Putting for peanuts. Lunch at the Shank Shop is always a thrill for newcomers. We have a miniature golf setup, and if you sink putts that have the little corresponding photos of a burger, dog, or grilled cheese, you get to eat the snack. If you choke the putts, no chow. It is this type of instant psychological feedback that has made Le Mondo so famous.

1 p.m. – Video magic. Few hackers realize the great contributions made by Bugs Bunny, The Three Stooges and W.C. Fields to the world of instructional golf. Viewing our classic tape collection imprints positive imagery on the inner memory. We have found great golfing secrets by freezing Bugs in motion. The famous three-fingered grip Bugs utilized is carefully studied by Mondo students.

3 p.m. – Water Hazard. Serious work on the inner memory. Campers settle in their ham-mocks surrounding tranquil Mondo Pond to think about playing a round of golf. We think shots and then tell them to our roomie/pro. He thinks about our thoughts and then thinks up some suggestions. Then we think about what he thought. The fast-paced ping-pong type of think/rethink method is the heart of the Mondo Theory.

The instant feedback makes for amazingly rapid progress. Soon, the golfer can think his way through an entire round. We think about sand-play, putting, chipping, irons, fairway woods and eventually the Big Thought — the driver.

6 p.m. — 19th hole. Cocktail hour at the fabulous Tee for Two combo lounge/pro shop. Here we work on the subconscious inner memory. Golfers sample the world-famous Duck Hook Fizz with a Divot back, and explore the lower levels of their golf psyche. Sometimes way down deep, we *know* we are better golfers than we *think* we are.

9 p.m. — Final Chapter. Le Mondo Inner Memory Golfing Club Cookout and Awards Ceremony. We all gather down by the Sand Trap barbecue pit. As the evening meal settles and the glow from the campfire bathes everyone in a flickering golden hue, we sing campfire golf songs: "Yankee Doodle Duffer," "Golftown Races," "It's a Long Way to Pebble Beach" and all the old favorites.

Now it's time for the awards. Who will win this year's coveted Mondo Cup, a finely crafted coffee mug, with a hand-painted depiction of tranquil Mondo

Pond? As is Mondo custom we let the campers decide who is the best inner memory golfer. By the time the fists stop flying, Le Mondo guests are usually ready to roll into their sleeping bags.

So ends another Mondo day. We take special pride in the unique experience shared by our campers. If you are ready to take the next step, you might be man enough for Mondo. Always remember the Mondo Motto:

"Playing well is never as important as *thinking* you play well."

Think about it.

14

The Case
Of the Four-Letter Word

The air in his office was as thick as U.S. Open rough. Shank was worried. The fan above his head creaked like a rusty old pull-cart. Something about his last case stunk, like the battered golf glove he kept in his drawer.

Maybe it was something she said. Or didn't say. That's the way it was for private golf detective Duff Shank. Things weren't always as they seemed. Sometimes a straight-in putt took a nasty curve.

The phone rang. Shank reached over with his seven iron and flipped the receiver into the air like a short chip shot. It landed softly in his hand.

"Fore," Shank muttered into the mouthpiece.

"I need help," whispered the female caller. Her voice was as silky as a Sam Snead backswing.

"You and everybody else," Shank shot back, "you should see my slice."

"I heard you can handle the heavy rough," the voice said with an edge of challenge.

She's good, Shank thought. And dangerous. About as much fun as a short pitch shot over a sand trap to a tight pin placement. Shank loved trouble shots.

He chewed thoughtfully on a wooden tee.

"Got yourself buried in a trap?" Shank asked.

"I'm in deep," she sighed, "my life isn't worth a divot. I need someone to check out a bad lie."

The grass shimmered in the morning sun like a shiny, cheap green suit.

Shank casually tossed a golf ball off his office wall and it ricocheted back into his face. He hid the pain.

"I'll putt around and see if anything drops," Shank said.

Pitching balls out his office window a few days later, Duff knew he needed to get away to think clearly. He headed for the driving range to watch the grotesque antics of men twisted and contorted in their futile efforts to hit a golf ball – hoping to solve the mystery of the game. Duff had seen it before. A thousand times. He had been there once himself. But that's another story. A long story, down an empty fairway,

Golf Detective Duff Shank searches for a clue . . .

that led to nowhere.

Shank had to concentrate. This was no easy matter, ever since he had choked that two-foot putt on the eighteenth green, on the day that changed his life forever.

The sense of failure and despair was heavy that day at the range. The atmosphere of futility usually gave Shank a lift, but today the case had his mind twisted and bent, like his last broken putter. Duff decided to walk along the first fairway. It was a crisp autumn day and the grass shimmered in the morning sun like a shiny, cheap, green suit – the kind of suit Shank was wearing.

Duff thought about the case. He had met with the voice on the phone and she had a tale to tell him that spun like a Trevino approach shot.

It seemed she had taken a golf wager. Shank knew the feeling. The condition of the bet was that she had one week to solve a small riddle, if she failed, she had to grant certain private playing privileges to the winner.

Clearly, it was an unplayable lie.

Fortunately, Shank liked riddles. Golf was a riddle, a game of possibilities that was impossible – like a Chinese finger trap, the more you tried to wiggle free the tighter the game gripped you.

Duff tried to clear his mind. It was clouded, as usual, by an endless stream of useless golf tips, swing keys and assorted golf items, that roamed unceasingly across the vast fairways of his mind. He was used to the drone, but lately his thoughts had taken on a British accent, and this really annoyed him.

Shank concentrated on the riddle. It was a simple word game. The problem was to name a word that spelled backward or forward meant a certain type of cruel torture.

The answer, Shank knew, was easier than a two-inch tap-in. But the real question was how could he get rid of the nasty duck-hook, which crept into his game at the worst times. He also wondered what the silky-voiced blonde would look like in golf shorts.

As for the riddle, the answer was what had tortured Shank for as long as he could remember. The word, of course, was GOLF, or spelled backwards FLOG, definitely two ways to inflict pain, thought Duff.

Too easy, but he had also thought the two-footer on the eighteenth green was easy, until it tailed off at the end and cost him the one true love of his life.

But that's another story.

Down a lonesome fairway that led to nowhere . . .

15

The Dating Game

Golf is sometimes like a blind date.

You show up at the links without your usual foursome and a "single" joins you.

"Singles" frighten me.

Who are they?

Where did they come from?

Why are they alone?

Playing with a "single" is the social crapshoot of sports — once the introductions are made, you're trapped. For better, or worse, you're going to spend the next four hours with a total stranger.

Sometimes, the outcome isn't pretty.

You may run into one of the strange life-forms that roam the fairways — watch out for these guys . . .

Spikers

You can tell this guy by the sound of his walk. If his spikes sort of slur across the cart path, you know you are in trouble. If your new partner packs more beer bottles than golf balls in his bag, things don't look good. When he tees it up, if he gets down on his knees and looks at the ground sideways to find a good spot, forget it. You are going to play a liquid round – things are going to be fluid.

Some golfers like to have good time and have a few beers during a round. Fine. But some spikers think the course is the local pub. I think their reasoning goes something like this:

"Well, hell, I didn't spend my afternoon in some dingy bar. I was out playing golf."

And wolfing back about twenty brewskis.

When you are playing golf with a spiker, be careful. Don't turn your back on the guy. He's got clubs, a hard little projectile, a power cart and a massive heat-on. Stir the situation with a few duffed shots and you are playing golf with a volcano. The best strategy for playing with spikers is heavy gambling. It gives them something to focus on, since they can't quite make out the ball or the hole. Make up a series of bets that are so confusing nobody understands the wager. Tell him he is a great golfer (spikers love this), then clean out his wallet.

Tipsters

You have just dumped one in the water on a short par three, over a small lake. You are not happy. Your new golf partner hits his shot thin, skips it off the water, bounces through the bunker onto the green. It is the

Make a wager that is so confusing that nobody understands the bet.

first green he has hit in regulation all day.

You go to the drop area, and as you are about to hit, your new pal says:

"You know, I think your problem is your grip."

You look at him. This guy hasn't hit a decent shot all day and now he's the club pro. But he has instilled a seed of doubt. Your grip, which has been the same for 15 years, starts to feel slightly uncomfortable. You get edgy, you look up on contact, and blade your shot into the bunker.

It seems that golf brings outs some deep hidden *need* to amuse.

"You looked up," he says.

You turn around, your eyes narrow, you take a full shoulder turn and whip the club through the hitting zone, which happens to be his head. He falls, you grab him by the neck and drag him into the pond. Your grip feels just fine as you hold him underwater until there is silence.

In my mind, I have killed many tipsters. They don't deserve to live. Most golfers play the game teetering on a very narrow mental cliff. We are insecure. We don't need a push over the edge. The game is impossible, but we have faith. Let us believe.

Tipsters are always lousy golfers. They have studied the game and have taken many lessons, but they are no good. Since nothing has worked for them, they use some strange logic to come to the conclusion that what didn't help them, will help you.

The best tactic for handling a tipster is violence. After his first bit of advice, make eye contact, hold the look about 30 long seconds and say calmly:

"If you say anything more about my golf game, I'll kill you."

If you look unbalanced and waggle the club in his direction he will usually shut up. If he docsn't, he must die.

Clowns

For some reason, a lot of golfers think they are funny. This is strange, since in their everyday life, at home or at the office, these same people have little, or no sense of humor. Somehow, hitting the links seems to transform normal people into comedians. It's an ugly sight.

It seems golf brings out some deep, hidden *need* to amuse. These clowns are possessed. They are relentless in their pursuit of laughs. Golf comics know about a billion jokes and are determined to get them all in during the round. These guys walk on the green and it's like someone handed them a mike.

"Hey, I just got a new set of clubs for my wife. It was a great trade."

"Wow, your golf swing is so ugly you should only play at night."

Funny stuff.

The only way to handle the course comic is to laugh. And don't stop. After the first joke, start to howl. Slap the clown on the back. Hard. Fall down. Roll around and go into hysterical convulsions. Pound the ground. Drool. Thrash and babble. Keep laughing. Usually five minutes is about all it takes to really frighten the jokester. If not, repeat the process with the next joke. If that doesn't work tell him the one about the funny golfer who got buried alive in a sand trap . . . it's a real killer.

16

Dig Deep

Sometimes in golf, it is the small things that really matter.

Like the divot.

This small chunk of earth has never been fully appreciated.

A good, full-bodied divot is a powerful, assertive statement. A fine rip in the fairway shows you are a golfer who is not afraid to dig deep and take a big bite out of life. You're a born leader, confident, and you command respect.

You're tough.

You know damn well you own a piece of earth and you're not bashful about staking a claim to your piece of the pie.

Unfortunately, some of us aren't so brave.

We have trouble letting go and releasing our pent-up power. We have a hard time being aggressive and hitting down and through the ball. We don't like to lose control.

We are careful. We choose to pick, or scoop at the ball. Daintily. We don't want to create an unsightly blemish in the turf. We take no divots, or at best, we manage shallow, thin affairs. Alas, much of our lives are spent in this manner – skimming the surface of existence – we don't take a slice out of life, so we slice the golf ball.

We are wimps.

But there is hope. The fearful need to examine their assumptions about the game of golf. Do we think golf is a nice game? Civilized? A pristine pastime for gentle souls? These ideas, of course, are nonsense.

And the divot becomes a philosophical statement. I take divots, therefore, I am.

Golf is cruel. The game is a beast. Golf is a savage, primitive affair, one step removed from cavemen bashing each other with clubs.

The game can smell fear. Golf will cut you out of the herd and hunt you down. So be prepared. You must learn to play like a warrior. No fear. No mercy.

Rip that turf. Let out the true golf *monster* that you really are. This is golf and life at its most basic. Here, we find the true nature of being. Here, at the moment of impact, we confront our essential nothingness.

Don't be afraid to take a bite out of life . . .

And the divot becomes a philosophical statement.

I take divots, therefore, I am.

The divot is such a simple, yet beautiful object. It is perfectly tangible. It either exists, or it doesn't. You either took one, or your didn't. The proof is right there. You either look down and see a finely etched hole in the earth or you see barren nothingness — the void, the total meaninglessness of your existence.

Ah, but if you see a firm slash in the turf you know what you have wrought is nearby — a fine piece of grass that proves you aren't afraid to leave your mark.

Now, you can complete your heroic journey. You replace your divot and the cycle is complete. Life and death on the links. You are one with the earth.

So let go. Dig in.

Remember, a divot not taken is an opportunity lost forever — so go out there and make the earth move.

17

Diamonds in the Rough

You are a special person.

You deserve the best.

You know what you like, and you aren't afraid to be different.

That is why you are receiving this letter.

We want to offer you a rare opportunity.

A chance to join our unique group. You have been chosen because we feel you are one of us. We know certain things about you.

We know you are a golfer.

And not just any golfer, but a student of the links – one who appreciates the history of the game.

You are a golf collector. You have a vast collection of clubs, balls, art, autographs, programs, books, medals, magazines, trophies, old tees, postcards, lighters, ash-trays – your home is a veritable golf museum.

But it isn't enough.

You feel a void.

You have many rare and expensive pieces, but you haven't really touched the legends of the links.

You want more.

Perhaps we can help.

Our organization has worked for decades to acquire items of such uniqueness and rarity that few collectors even know they exist.

The mission of our society has always been clear — to seek out golf artifacts that have a common thread — every item we accept has been personally touched, used or created by a golf legend.

We want to "feel" the presence of greatness.

To build such a collection was a monumental task. We have paid enormous sums to a vast underground network of caddies, tournament officials, groundskeepers, and countless others to obtain these treasures.

Now, *you* have a chance to "touch" a legend.

We present — *The Collection.*

You will notice that although we describe the items for sale in great detail, we have not included a price. We know if there is an item you MUST have, price will be no object. The following is a small sample of our current stock.

Tobacco Collection

Many golfers collect cards from tobacco packs as well as other cigarette related ephemera. We offer something more personal and unique.

Cigarette Butts

These are the actual butts from cigarettes smoked by

A fine cigarette butt makes a great collectible . . .

the greats during tournament play. These treasures were carefully retrieved and preserved by our network of caddies. Each butt is numbered and labeled by player, date and tournament and comes with a letter of authenticity. The butts are handsomely displayed in a vintage leather cigarette box. All the butts are strictly graded from good to mint. A good butt will show some abuse, may be faded, and have significant tobacco loss. A mint butt will look almost new, with snow white paper, no rips or tears and with all the unused tobacco still intact.

> Each hair sample is dated and guaranteed to be "game used."

We offer butts from all the legends, Hogan, Sarazen, Arnie, as well as an extensive collection of butts from cigarettes smoked at all the major championships.

Some of our clients like to collect player butts, others seek to get one butt from every major tournament. Others seek rare historically significant butts, such as a '61 Palmer or a '48 Hogan butt.

We also have a very limited stock of cigar butts.

Truly scarce, is our offering of unopened packs. These are cigarettes in boxes that were actually in the bag of a great during tournament play but never smoked. Imagine owning a Lucky Strike pack that was in Hogan's bag during the '52 Masters!

Divots

We are the only known organization that has had the foresight to understand the rarity of a divot taken by a great golf legend. For almost a century, we have been secretly bribing caddies, groundskeepers and tournament officials to obtain these rarities.

Caddies had to actually smuggle in pieces of turf and secretly switch the pieces of sod to acquire these priceless pieces of history.

We offer divots off the clubs of all the greats. Many collectors like to have one divot from each of their favorite players so they can compare the texture and depth of these magnificent specimens. Many collectors seek historically significant divots. Imagine having a Nicklaus divot from his first major championship!

Each divot is listed by player, tournament, hole and shot. The divots have been preserved by a secret technique created by our staff of scientists and are displayed in a revolving glass container shaped like a golf ball.

Personal Collection

For some collectors, only the best will do. Some of us want to touch our heros. Our *Personal* section offers a chance to own a real piece of a legend.

We are privileged to offer the finest assortment of legendary hair in existence. Remember, this is not only hair from the head of a golf great, it is the actual hair that was growing on his head *while he was playing a major tournament.* Each hair sample is dated and guaranteed to be "game used."

We have strands of hair that were growing on Bobby Jones' head during the final tournament of his Grand Slam. We have Byron Nelson hair from his record-setting year, slicked-down Hagen hair from a historic PGA victory, Watson hair from one of his British Open wins, and other samples from just about every great player during all the major championships.

The hair strands are preserved in a small test tube which has been tastefully framed with a picture of the golf legend and an autograph.

We'd like to thank you for allowing us to present *The Collection.* Please contact us if we can help with your collecting needs. Of course, we are also avid buyers of unique items. Currently, we are adding to our gum collection. If you have any samples of gum that was chewed by a notable golfer during tournament play, we are actively *buying!*

18

Praise the Links

Dear friends, this is the Reverend Jimmy Joe Hooker, welcoming you to join hearts with us at the Everlasting Church of the Links. Yes, brothers and sisters we have come together to spread the Truth. And the Truth is this.

Golf is the key to salvation.

Yes, brothers and sisters, the way of *Golf* is the path of the righteous man. And I say unto you, he that hath no clubs, shall never drive his way into the fairway of heaven.

Say Amen.

It was revealed to me, the Rev. Jimmy Joe, that the Garden of Eden was yes, verily a *Golf Course*. A lush championship spread. And the forbidden fruit was not an apple but a Pear, or as we southerners say, a *Par*.

Do you follow me brothers and sisters? Say Amen.

So God created a *Golf Course* and he tempted Adam

(the first duffer) with *Par*.

And friends, we have been in the deep rough since that day. Seeking *Par*, doomed to the eternal hell of bogey.

My fellow duffers do you hear me?

We must come to know, in our hearts, that *Golf* is the Answer. Brothers and Sisters let us look at the *Truths of Golf* so we can better see. Say Amen.

1. Keep Thy Head Down.
Be a humble duffer. Know that there are greater forces at work on the Course. Don't look up until after your shot flies — don't be anxious to see the fruits of thy labors. Be cool.

2. Play it as it Lay.
Take life as it comes. In every life there are divots, buried lies, deep rough and potential hazards. Remember, life isn't a bowl of cherries, it's a small bucket of range balls.

3. Slow Play is a Sin.
We aren't here to dawdle. Be about your work and move on. *Golf* is not practice — it is life. So hustle.

4. Replace Thy Divots.
The Course is for all mankind so treat it well. This is a parable of life and death. Don't dig your own grave. Be tidy.

5. Keep Honestly Thy Scorecard.
Yes, someone is keeping score. This isn't a free ride.

Honestly keep thy scorecard.

Everything you do on the Course is noted. Paranoia is an appropriate response to the game. Be careful.

Yes friends, you see now that the way of *Golf* is the way of mankind. And I, the Rev. Jimmy Joe, want to lead the march down the center of the fairway of life.

Brothers and sisters, I have had a vision. I see the world joined in a great brotherhood of *Golf*. Great green Courses covering the globe. Missionaries spreading the Word of *Golf* to the most remote regions of the world. Our hands reaching out and placing a putter into the hand of every innocent child.

Friends, I need your help. The Everlasting Church of the Links wants you to become a partner in this great Golfing Crusade. I can hear you talking out there. You are saying, I want to help Rev. Jimmy Joe, but my own green fees are so high and I need some new Pings.

I, the Rev. Jimmy Joe, hear you. I know the path down the links is an arduous one. But we must sacrifice.

Brothers and sisters, some of the flock say unto me.

"Rev. Jimmy Joe, why do you have expensive memberships at exclusive private clubs, and hundreds of sets of gold plated clubs and a nine hole course in

---◆---

L ife isn't a bowl of cherries, it's a small bucket of range balls.

---◆---

your backyard."

And I say unto them.

"Quiet, I'm putting."

And they *understand.*

So friends, join with us and send your check now and receive a handsome bag of tees blessed by me, the Rev. Jimmy Joe.

Brothers and sisters let us raise our voices together in a mighty chorus that will ring down the fairways of heaven.

Yes, Yessss, Swing low sweet backswing, Jimmy Joe gonna carry you home . . . Swing low sweet backswing, Jimmy Joe gonna carry you home . . . So remember, friends, when you shank one into the trees, blow a two foot putt or chilly dip a short chip, I, the Rev. Jimmy Joe Hooker, will be praying for you. Keep your head down and send in those old scorecards with your generous donations.

May all of your putts fall.

Say Amen.

Epilogue

Don't Be Cruel

Sometimes I'm not sure it really happened. It does seem impossible, but then, who knows what really is possible?

All I know is that one day a few years back I went out to my usual golfing haunt and there he was, standing on the first tee, taking some practice swings, waiting for a playing partner.

It was an awesome sight – he seemed to glow in the golden light of the early morning sun. His practice swings left a shiny silver trail as they cut through the still air.

I blinked my eyes to make sure he wouldn't disappear. But he was really there.

The King.

I was going to play a round of golf with Elvis.

In a way, this was an answer to my prayers. Ever since I took up golf there was one question that always troubled me.

Did Elvis golf?

There is very little documentation to support the theory that Elvis had ever packed a bag. This, of course, upset me because if Elvis didn't play the game, maybe golf wasn't cool.

But now my question was answered.

Elvis stood before me, shimmering in a rhinestone Vegas jumpsuit, replete with cape and silk scarfs dangling from his neck. He had a bagful of old Hogan blades and woods. His putter appeared to be solid gold.

Elvis had already teed up his ball as I approached. He looked at me and nodded.

What happened next is hard to believe.

Elvis' pre-shot routine was dazzling.

You've never seen anyone waggle until you've seen the King.

His knees started flapping, his hip were grinding and he began swinging the club in a huge circle, like he was strumming a giant guitar.

Elvis was building up some terrifying coiled power.

He gave one last hip thrust. He looked at the ball and muttered.

"Don't be cruel."

And then he unleashed the pent-up energy into his shot and the ball blazed off the club screaming about 375 yards down the fairway. As the ball shot out of sight, Elvis dropped to one knee and thrust out his fist like a karate punch.

"Wow," I said. "Nice shot."

Elvis looked up and mumbled in a low voice, "Thank you very much."

Some of the King's magic must have rubbed off on me because I hit a decent drive right down the middle.

So the King and I were off.

Elvis was a fast player. When he got to his shot, he quickly went through his prodigious waggle, then let it fly. The results were awesome. On the first five holes he had birdie putts of no more than six feet. He sank them all.

The putting greens were like a stage for Elvis. He held his gold putter like a mike and prowled around, lining up his putt — the hound dog was loose. When he was ready to go, he approached the ball from the back, did a 360 spin, gave two quick karate kicks, and then quickly stroked the ball dead in the heart.

By the seventh hole, Elvis was eight under, having eagled the sixth. He hadn't said a word to me since the first hole.

I was in a trance. The King's amazing play had left me stunned. But through the fog, I knew I had to summon the courage to ask Elvis the secret to his magical game.

Finally on the tenth hole, after yet another Elvis birdie, I asked meekly.

"I was wondering if you had any tips that might help my game?"

Elvis looked at me. I think he had forgotten I was even there. His eyes lowered to the ground and he muttered.

"Hips and hair."

"Oh," I said.

He looked straight into my eyes.

"Son, move your hips. Don't move your hair," he drawled.

He walked over to his ball and I knew the lesson was over.

For the rest of the round I studied the Elvis method. Although his body seemed to be gyrating all over the place, he practiced what he preached. His hair, which was swept back like a huge helmet, never moved.

Elvis shot a 58 that day. It was the greatest round of golf I had ever seen. On the last hole, as we were walking off the green, I couldn't help but take one last shot.

"Elvis, how'd you possibly shoot a 58?" I asked.

He looked at me, his upper lip curled and he said.

"I did it my way."

Golf Treasures

The author is a member of the International Golf Collectors Society and actively buys and sells golf memorabilia.

If you have any unique vintage golf items you'd like to sell, we are interested.

If you are looking for a very special gift for a golfer, perhaps we can help. We have items that range from inexpensive decoration pieces to very rare one of a kind treasures.

Please contact us with any questions you might have.

Steve Webber
P.O. Box 6823
San Mateo, CA 94403
(650) 347-6890

Order Form

Ship To:

Name: _____

Address: _____

City: _____

State: _____ Zip:_____

Phone: (_____) _____

                                    Quantity   Amount

Bogey Blues, Tales of Golf Madness   _____   _____
Prices: 1 book, $10.95;
          2 books, $19.95;
          5 books, $45.00
          call for volume discounts (650) 737 8233

               CA residents add 8.25% sales tax   _____

Shipping add $2 for first book, $1 ea. additional book   _____

                              TOTAL   _____

Please send **check or money order** to:

       Gray Eagle Publishing
       P.O. Box 6905
       San Mateo, CA 94403

Please expect 2-4 weeks delivery time.